A NATURE POEM FOR
EVERY SPRING EVENING

A NATURE POEM FOR EVERY SPRING EVENING

EDITED BY *Jane McMorland Hunter*

BATSFORD

First published in the United Kingdom in 2023 by
B.T. Batsford Ltd
43 Great Ormond Street
London WC1N 3HZ
An imprint of B.T. Batsford Holdings Ltd

ISBN 9781849948173

A CIP catalogue record for this book is available from the
British Library.

10 9 8 7 6 5 4 3 2 1
33 32 31 30 29 28 27 26 25 24 23

Reproduction by Mission Productions, Hong Kong
Printed by Toppan Leefung Printing Ltd, China

This book can be ordered direct from the publisher at
www.batsfordbooks.com

CONTENTS

To Matilda, who came home. And to Mat
and Sarah, who helped. With all my love.

ABOUT THE EDITOR

Jane McMorland Hunter has compiled
12 anthologies of poetry for Batsford and the
National Trust. She also writes gardening and
cookery books and works as a gardener and at
Hatchards bookshop in Piccadilly. She lives in
London with a small, grey tabby cat.

Introduction

The arrival of spring sees the natural world beginning to awaken. As the season progresses the days get noticeably longer, with evenings that we can all enjoy. Dusk no longer takes hold at tea-time, and it seems as if we all have a little more time. Time which you can use to enjoy a daily poem, either sitting by a roaring fire or outside enjoying the last warm rays of sunshine.

Spring is a season much loved by poets and, as with the other seasons of the year, I am convinced that there is a real spring and an imagined or literary one. Early spring can be cold with weather more fitting for winter, but in poetry and in many of our memories it becomes the time of fluffy lambs, delicate blossom and heartening birdsong.

At this time of year the light changes, not just in poetic terms but also in reality. Towards the end of March those of us in the northern hemisphere have the spring or vernal equinox. This is the moment when everything in the natural world changes. From now on the days lengthen, there is more light, even if not yet more warmth, and it is this light that marks spring. Along with the lengthening days, spring has a quality of light that brings hope and the promise of summer to come. As described by Emily Dickinson, it is a light we feel more than see – fleeting but unmistakeable.

Green is the colour of early spring: the apple green of D. H. Lawrence and the green linnet of William Wordsworth, which slip towards gold as the spring progresses with Christina Rossetti's buttercups, marigolds, waterside flags, cowslips and gorse. Among the greens and golds there is blossom, beloved of A. E. Housman, Ethelwyn Wetherald and William Blake with cherries 'hung with snow', apple blossoms 'trembling into birth' to the point where 'every Tree / And Flower and Herb soon fill the air with an innumerable dance,' respectively.

While March is known for its winds, April is renowned for its showers, which eventually allow May to burst into flower. It is in April that we begin to appreciate the sounds of spring: the nightingale, the lark and the cuckoo in particular. At the same time the colours of the season begin to change too: bluebells like 'smoke held down by frost' followed by lilac near a church clock set at ten to three and the pale and delicate lily of the valley. Dandelions may be an unwanted weed for many but for Walt Whitman they are innocent and golden, emerging 'simple and fresh and fair' at winter's close.

Several poems in this collection are written by war poets, specifically those of the First World War. For all of them the joy of spring stood in stark contrast to the horror of the battlefields, the signs of nature emerging from winter regardless of the fighting. Edward Thomas, Laurence Binyon, Edmund Blunden and Humbert Wolfe all saw the destruction and devastation of war both in natural and human terms. Not all their poems here were written during the war, or are even directly about it, but their vivid descriptions of birdsong and wayside flowers cannot but remind us of the disparity between nature and the harsh reality of war.

The women who wrote at this time viewed spring slightly differently, theirs is more a view of what is lost, rather than a direct comparison. Poets such as Sara Teasdale recognized that nature does not care if mankind perishes: 'And Spring herself, when she woke at dawn / Would scarcely know that we were gone.' Charlotte Mew too acknowledges that whatever destruction we may cause, the rain, the sky, the sea breeze and the sun will again come to heal the earth and enable the spring to return. But some losses can never be recovered; E. Nesbit knows the magic of spring will return but with the rows of little black crosses it will never be quite the same. Nearly all the poets writing during wartime write Spring rather than spring. Many other poets do at other times, but here it seems particularly apt; the season is something greater than all of mankind.

Even with the lengthening days spring feels like a fleeting season. At its start it has the ponderous feel of winter, by the end it is speeding towards summer. The important thing is not to miss it. Whether one has five or fifty years A. E. Housman's words ring true:

> And since to look at things in bloom
> Fifty springs are little room,
> About the woodlands I will go
> To see the cherry hung with snow.

(From 'The Loveliest of Trees', *A Shropshire Lad*)

MARCH

Green Leaves and Blossoms

1ST MARCH

March, You Old Blusterer

March, you old blusterer,
  What will you bring?
Sunny days, stormy days,
  Under your wing?
No matter which it be,
  You will bring spring.

Whether Lion roaring comes
  Over bleak hills,
Whether Lamb bleating goes
  Seeking sweet rills,
You will bring primroses
  And daffodils.

Whether the earth shows a
  White or green quilt,
Where in both hedge and tree
  Men hear a lilt,
March, you old blusterer
  Nests will be built.

Eleanor Farjeon (1881–1965)

2ND MARCH

To Primroses Fill'd With Morning-dew

Why doe ye weep, sweet Babes? can Tears
        Speak griefe in you,
        Who were but borne
    Just as the modest Morne
      Teem'd her refreshing dew?
Alas you have not known that shower,
        That marres a flower;
        Nor felt th'unkind
      Breath of a blasting wind;
      Nor are ye worne with yeares;
        Or warpt, as we,
      Who think it strange to see,
Such pretty flowers, (like to Orphans young)
To speak by Teares, before ye have a Tongue.

Speak, whimp'ring Younglings, and make known
        The reason, why
        Ye droop, and weep;
      Is it for want of sleep?
      Or childish Lullabie?
    Or that ye have not seen as yet

The *Violet?*
    Or brought a kisse
From that Sweet-heart to this?
No, no, this sorrow shown
    By your teares shed
Wo'd have this Lecture read,
That things of greatest, so of meanest worth,
Conceiv'd with grief are, and with teares brought
                        forth.

Robert Herrick (1591–1674)

3RD MARCH

It Came With the Year's First Crocus

PRAELUDIUM, IV

It came with the year's first crocus
   In a world of winds and snows –
Because it would, because it must,
Because of life and time and lust;
And a year's first crocus served my turn
   As well as the year's first rose.

The March rack hurries and hectors,
   The March dust heaps and blows;
But the primrose flouts the daffodil,
And here's the patient violet still;
And the year's first crocus brought me luck,
   So hey for the year's first rose!

W. E. Henley (1849–1903)

4TH MARCH

Early Spring

I

Once more the Heavenly Power
   Makes all things new,
And domes the red-plow'd hills
   With loving blue;
The blackbirds have their wills,
   The throstles too.

II

Opens a door in Heaven;
   From skies of glass
A Jacob's ladder falls
   On greening grass,
And o'er the mountain-walls
   Young angels pass.

III

Before them fleets the shower,
   And burst the buds,
And shine the level lands,
   And flash the floods;
The stars are from their hands
   Flung thro' the woods,

23

IV

The woods with living airs
   How softly fann'd,
Light airs from where the deep,
   All down the sand,
Is breathing in his sleep,
   Heard by the land.

V

O follow, leaping blood,
   The season's lure!
O heart, look down and up
   Serene, secure,
Warm as the crocus cup,
   Like snow-drops, pure!

Alfred, Lord Tennyson (1809–1892)

5TH MARCH

A Thrush in the Trenches

FROM *THE SOLDIER*

Suddenly he sang across the trenches,
   vivid in the fleeting hush
as a star-shell through the smashed black branches,
   a more than English thrush.

Suddenly he sang, and those who listened
   nor moved nor wondered, but
heard, all bewitched, the sweet unhastened
   crystal Magnificat.

One crouched, a muddied rifle clasping,
   and one a filled grenade,
but little cared they, while he went lisping
   the one clear tune he had.

Paused horror, hate and Hell a moment,
   (you could almost hear the sigh)
and still he sang to them, and so went
   (suddenly) singing by.

Humbert Wolfe (1885–1940)

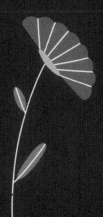

6TH MARCH

Spring Night

Through the smothered air the wicker finds
A muttering voice, 'crick' cries the embered ash.
Sharp rains knap at the panes beyond the blinds,
The flues and eaves moan, the jarred windows clash;
And like a sea breaking its barriers, flooding
New green abysses with untold uproar.
The cataract nightwind whelms the time of budding.
Swooping in sightless fury off the moor
Into our valley. Not a star shines. Who
Would guess the martin and the cuckoo come,
The pear in bloom, the bloom gone from the plum.
The cowslips countless as a morning dew?
So mad it blows, so truceless and so grim.
As if day's host of flowers were a moment's whim.

Edmund Blunden (1896–1974)

7TH MARCH

Answer to a Child's Question

Do you ask what the birds say? The Sparrow, the
  Dove,
The Linnet and Thrush say, 'I love and I love!'
In the winter they're silent – the wind is so strong;
What it says, I don't know, but it sings a loud song.
But green leaves, and blossoms, and sunny warm
  weather,
And singing, and loving – all come back together.
But the Lark is so brimful of gladness and love,
The green fields below him, the blue sky above,
That he sings, and he sings; and forever sings he –
'I love my Love, and my Love loves me!'

Samuel Taylor Coleridge (1772–1834)

8TH MARCH

Very Early Spring

The fields are snowbound no longer;
There are little blue lakes and flags of tenderest
  green.
The snow has been caught up into the sky –
So many white clouds – and the blue of the sky is
  cold.
Now the sun walks in the forest,
He touches the bows and stems with his golden
  fingers;
They shiver, and wake from slumber.
Over the barren branches he shakes his yellow
  curls.
Yet is the forest full of the sound of tears ...
A wind dances over the fields.
Shrill and clear the sound of her waking laughter,
Yet the little blue lakes tremble
And the flags of tenderest green bend and quiver.

Katherine Mansfield (1888–1923)

9TH MARCH

Hark! 'Tis the Thrush,
Undaunted, Undeprest

Hark! 'tis the Thrush, undaunted, undeprest,
By twilight premature of cloud and rain;
Nor does that roaring wind deaden his strain
Who carols thinking of his Love and nest,
And seems, as more incited, still more blest.
Thanks; thou hast snapped a fire-side Prisoner's
    chain,
Exulting Warbler! eased a fretted brain,
And in a moment charmed my cares to rest.
Yes, I will forth, bold Bird! and front the blast,
That we may sing together, if thou wilt,
So loud, so clear, my Partner through life's day,
Mute in her nest love-chosen, if not love-built
Like thine, shall gladden, as in seasons past,
Thrilled by loose snatches of the social Lay.

William Wordsworth (1770–1850)

10ᵀᴴ MARCH

A Light Exists in Spring

A Light exists in Spring
Not present on the Year
At any other period –
When March is scarcely here

A Color stands abroad
On Solitary Fields
That Science cannot overtake
But Human Nature feels.

It waits upon the Lawn,
It shows the furthest Tree
Upon the furthest Slope you know
It almost speaks to you.

Then as Horizons step
Or Noons report away
Without the Formula of sound
It passes and we stay –

A quality of loss
Affecting our Content
As Trade had suddenly encroached
Upon a Sacrament.

Emily Dickinson (1830–1886)

11TH MARCH

A Forest Lake

O lake of sylvan shore! when gentle Spring
Slopes down upon thee from the mountain side,
When birds begin to build and brood and sing;
Or, in maturer season, when the pied
And fragrant turf is throng'd with blossoms rare;
In the frore sweetness of the breathing morn,
When the loud echoes of the herdsman's horn
Do sally forth upon the silent air
Of thy thick forestry, may I be there,
While the wood waits to see its phantom born
At clearing twilight, in thy grassy breast;
Or, when cool eve is busy, on thy shores,
With trails of purple shadow from the West,
Or dusking in the wake of tardy oars.

Charles Tennyson Turner (1808–1879)

12TH MARCH

Green

The dawn was apple-green,
   The sky was green wine held up in the sun,
The moon was a golden petal between.

She opened her eyes, and green
   They shone, clear like flowers undone
For the first time, now for the first time seen.

D. H. Lawrence (1885–1930)

13TH MARCH

There Was an Old Man in a Tree

There was an Old Man in a tree,
Whose whiskers were lovely to see;
But the birds of the air pluck'd them perfectly bare,
To make themselves nests in that tree.

Edward Lear (1812–1888)

14TH MARCH

The Soul of Love

FROM *SPRING, THE SEASONS*

When first the soul of love is sent abroad,
Warm through the vital air, and on the heart
Harmonious seizes, the gay troops begin,
In gallant thought, to plume the painted wing,
And try again the long-forgotten strain;
At first faint-warbled: but no sooner grows
The soft infusion prevalent, and wide,
Than, all alive, at once their joy o'erflows
In music unconfined. Up springs the lark,
Shrill-voiced, and loud, the messenger of morn;
Ere yet the shadows fly, he mounted sings
Amid the dawning clouds, and from their haunts
Calls up the tuneful nations. Every copse
Deep-tangled, tree irregular, and bush
Bending with dewy moisture, o'er the heads
Of the coy choristers that lodge within,
Are prodigal of harmony. The thrush
And wood-lark, o'er the kind contending throng
Superior heard, run through the sweetest length
Of notes; when listening Philomela deigns
To let them joy, and purposes, in thought
Elate, to make her night excel their day.

James Thomson (1700–1748)

15ᵀᴴ MARCH

Soil

On this day, the breathing earth
gave this little primrose birth.
On this day the living soil
yielded up its golden spoil.
Engaged in such a noble toil,
who despises simple soil?

David Austin (1926–2018)

16TH MARCH

The Dalliance of the Eagles

Skirting the river road, (my forenoon walk, my
  rest,)
Skyward in air a sudden muffled sound, the
  dalliance of the eagles,
The rushing amorous contact high in space together,
The clinching interlocking claws, a living, fierce,
  gyrating wheel,
Four beating wings, two beaks, a swirling mass
  tight grappling,
In tumbling turning clustering loops, straight
  downward falling,
Till o'er the river pois'd, the twain yet one, a
  moment's lull,
A motionless still balance in the air, then parting,
  talons loosing,
Upward again on slow-firm pinions slanting, their
  separate diverse flight,
She hers, he his, pursuing.

Walt Whitman (1819–1892)

17TH MARCH

But These Things Also

But these things also are Spring's –
On banks by the roadside the grass
Long-dead that is greyer now
Than all the Winter it was;

The shell of a little snail bleached
In the grass; chip of flint, and mite
Of chalk; and the small birds' dung
In splashes of purest white:

All the white things a man mistakes
For earliest violets
Who seeks through Winter's ruins
Something to pay Winter's debts,

While the North blows, and starling flocks
By chattering on and on
Keep their spirits up in the mist,
And Spring's here, Winter's not gone.

Edward Thomas (1878–1917)

18TH MARCH

Four Ducks on a Pond

Four ducks on a pond,
A grass-bank beyond,
A blue sky of spring,
White clouds on the wing;
What a little thing
To remember for years –
To remember with tears!

William Allingham (1824–1889)

19ᵀᴴ MARCH

There Will Come Soft Rains

(WAR TIME)

There will come soft rains and the smell of the ground,
And swallows circling with their shimmering sound;

And frogs in the pools singing at night,
And wild-plum trees in tremulous white;

Robins will wear their feathery fire,
Whistling their whims on a low fence-wire;

And not one will know of the war, not one
Will care at last when it is done.

Not one would mind, neither bird nor tree,
If mankind perished utterly;

And Spring herself, when she woke at dawn
Would scarcely know that we were gone.

Sara Teasdale (1884–1933)

20TH MARCH

The Fish

In a cool curving world he lies
And ripples with dark ecstasies.
The kind luxurious lapse and steal
Shapes all his universe to feel
And know and be; the clinging stream
Closes his memory, glooms his dream,
Who lips the roots o' the shore, and glides
Superb on unreturning tides.
Those silent waters weave for him
A fluctuant mutable world and dim,
Where wavering masses bulge and gape
Mysterious, and shape to shape
Dies momently through whorl and hollow,
And form and line and solid follow
Solid and line and form to dream
Fantastic down the eternal stream;
An obscure world, a shifting world,
Bulbous, or pulled to thin, or curled,
Or serpentine, or driving arrows,
Or serene slidings, or March narrows.
There slipping wave and shore are one,

And weed and mud. No ray of sun,
But glow to glow fades down the deep
(As dream to unknown dream in sleep);
Shaken translucency illumes
The hyaline of drifting glooms;
The strange soft-handed depth subdues
Drowned colour there, but black to hues,
As death to living, decomposes –
Red darkness of the heart of roses,
Blue brilliant from dead starless skies,
And gold that lies behind the eyes,
The unknown unnameable sightless white
That is the essential flame of night,
Lustreless purple, hooded green,
The myriad hues that lie between
Darkness and darkness! ...

Rupert Brooke (1887–1915)

21ˢᵀ MARCH

I Watched a Blackbird

I watched a blackbird on a budding sycamore
One Easter Day, when sap was stirring twigs to
the core;
I saw his tongue, and crocus-coloured bill
Parting and closing as he turned his trill;
Then he flew down, seized on a stem of hay,
And upped to where his building scheme was
under way,
As if so sure a nest were never shaped on spray.

Thomas Hardy (1840–1928)

22ᴺᴰ MARCH

To Violets

Welcome, Maids of Honour,
    You doe bring
    In the Spring;
And wait upon her.

She has Virgins many,
    Fresh and faire;
    Yet you are
More sweet than any.

Y'are the Maiden Posies;
    And so grac't,
    To be plac't,
'Fore Damask Roses.

Yet, though thus respected,
    By and by
    Ye doe lie,
Poore Girles, neglected.

Robert Herrick (1591–1674)

23RD MARCH

To a Cat

Stately, kindly, lordly friend,
  Condescend
Here to sit by me, and turn
Glorious eyes that smile and burn,
Golden eyes, love's lustrous meed,
On the golden page I read.

All your wondrous wealth of hair,
  Dark and fair,
Silken-shaggy, soft and bright
As the clouds and beams of night,
Pays my reverent hand's caress
Back with friendlier gentleness.

Dogs may fawn on all and some
  As they come;
You, a friend of loftier mind,
Answer friends alone in kind.
Just your foot upon my hand
Softly bids it understand.

Algernon Charles Swinburne (1837–1909)

24TH MARCH

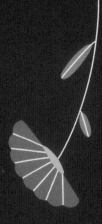

The Enkindled Spring

This spring as it comes bursts up in bonfires green,
Wild puffing of green-fire trees, and flame-filled
    bushes,
Thorn-blossom lifting in wreaths of smoke between
Where the wood fumes up and the flickering, watery
    rushes.

I am amazed at this spring, this conflagration
Of green fires lit on the soil of the earth, this blaze
Of growing, these smoke-puffs that puff in wild
    gyration,
Faces of people blowing across my gaze!

And I, what sort of fire am I among
This conflagration of spring? the gap in it all – !
Not even palish smoke like the rest of the throng.
Less than the wind that runs to the flamy call!

D. H. Lawrence (1885–1930)

25TH MARCH

The Fields of Flanders

Last year the fields were all glad and gay
With silver daisies and silver may;
There were kingcups gold by the river's edge
And primrose stars under every hedge.

This year the fields are trampled and brown,
The hedges are broken and beaten down,
And where the primroses used to grow
Are little black crosses set in a row.

And the flower of hopes, and the flower of dreams,
The noble, fruitful, beautiful schemes,
The tree of life with its fruit and bud,
Are trampled down in the mud and the blood.

The changing seasons will bring again
The magic of Spring to our wood and plain:
Though the Spring be so green as never was seen
The crosses will still be black in the green.

The God of battles shall judge the foe
Who trampled our country and laid her low ...
God! hold our hands on the reckoning day,
Lest all we owe them we should repay.

E. Nesbit (1858–1924)

26TH MARCH

The Blackbird

Ov all the birds upon the wing
Between the zunny show'rs o' spring, –
Vor all the lark, a-swingèn high,
Mid zing below a cloudless sky,
An' sparrows, clust'rèn roun' the bough,
Mid chatter to the men at plough, –
The blackbird, whisslèn in among
The boughs, do zing the gaÿest zong.

Vor we do hear the blackbird zing
His sweetest ditties in the spring,
When nippèn win's noo mwore do blow
Vrom northern skies, wi' sleet or snow,
But drēve light doust along between
The leäne-zide hedges, thick an' green;
An' zoo the blackbird in among
The boughs do zing the gaÿest zong.

'Tis blithe, wi' newly-open'd eyes,
To zee the mornèn's ruddy skies;
Or, out a-haulèn frith or lops
Vrom new-plēshed hedge or new-vell'd copse,
To rest at noon in primrwose beds
Below the white-bark'd woak-trees' heads;
But there's noo time, the whole daÿ long,
Lik' evenèn wi' the blackbird's zong.

William Barnes (1801–1886)

27TH MARCH

Little Gidding

Midwinter spring is its own season
Sempiternal though sodden towards sundown,
Suspended in time, between pole and tropic.
When the short day is brightest, with frost and fire,
The brief sun flames the ice, on pond and ditches,
In windless cold that is the heart's heat,
Reflecting in a watery mirror
A glare that is blindness in the early afternoon.
And glow more intense than blaze of branch, or
  brazier,
Stirs the dumb spirit: no wind, but pentecostal fire
In the dark time of the year. Between melting and
  freezing
The soul's sap quivers. There is no earth smell
Or smell of living thing. This is the spring time
But not in time's covenant. Now the hedgerow
Is blanched for an hour with transitory blossom
Of snow, a bloom more sudden
Than that of summer, neither budding nor fading,
Not in the scheme of generation.
Where is the summer, the unimaginable
Zero summer?

T. S. Eliot (1888–1965)

28TH MARCH

Night-piece

Now independent, beautiful and proud,
Out of the vanishing body of a cloud
Like its arisen soul the full moon swims
Over the sea, into whose distant brims
Has flowed the last of the light. I am alone.
Even the diving gannet now is flown
From these unpeopled sands. A mist lies cold
Upon the muffled boundaries of the world.
The lovely earth whose silence is so deep
Is folded up in the night, but not in sleep.

Eleanor Farjeon (1881–1965)

29TH MARCH

The Progress of Spring

The groundflame of the crocus breaks the mould,
    Fair Spring slides hither o'er the Southern sea,
Wavers on her thin stem the snowdrop cold
    That trembles not to kisses of the bee:
Come, Spring, for now from all the dripping eaves
    The spear of ice has wept itself away,
And hour by hour unfolding woodbine leaves
    O'er his uncertain shadow droops the day.
She comes! The loosen'd rivulets run;
    The frost-bead melts upon her golden hair;
Her mantle, slowly greening in the Sun,
    Now wraps her close, now arching leaves her bare
    To breaths of balmier air.

Up leaps the lark, gone wild to welcome her,
    About her glance the tits, and shriek the jays,
Before her skims the jubilant woodpecker,
    The linnet's bosom blushes at her gaze,

While round her brows a woodland culver flits,
  Watching her large light eyes and gracious
                                looks,
And in her open palm a halcyon sits
  Patient – the secret splendour of the brooks.
Come, Spring! She comes on waste and wood,
  On farm and field: but enter also here,
Diffuse thyself at will thro' all my blood,
  And, tho' thy violet sicken into sere,
    Lodge with me all the year!

Alfred, Lord Tennyson (1809–1892)

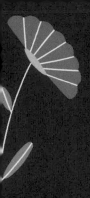

30TH MARCH

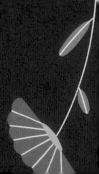

Stars, I Have Seen Them Fall

Stars, I have seen them fall,
  But when they drop and die
No star is lost at all
  From all the star-sown sky.
The toil of all that be
  Helps not the primal fault;
It rains into the sea,
  And still the sea is salt.

A. E. Housman (1859–1936)

31ST MARCH

The Beech-Tree's Petition

O leave this barren spot to me!
Spare, woodman, spare the beechen tree!
Though bush or floweret never grow
My dark unwarming shade below;
Nor summer bud perfume the dew
Of rosy blush, or yellow hue;
Nor fruits of autumn, blossom-born,
My green and glossy leaves adorn;
Nor murmuring tribes from me derive
The ambrosial amber of the hive;
Yet leave this barren spot to me:
Spare, woodman, spare the beechen tree!

Thrice twenty summers I have seen
The sky grow bright, the forest green;
And many a wintry wind have stood
In bloomless, fruitless solitude,
Since childhood in my pleasant bower
First spent its sweet and sportive hour,
Since youthful lovers in my shade
Their vows of truth and rapture made;

And on my trunk's surviving frame
Carved many a long-forgotten name.
Oh! by the sighs of gentle sound,
First breathed upon this sacred ground;
By all that Love has whispered here,
Or Beauty heard with ravished ear;
As Love's own altar honour me:
Spare, woodman, spare the beechen tree!

Thomas Campbell (1777–1844)

APRIL

The Nightingale Begins its Song

1ST APRIL

Home Thoughts From Abroad

I

Oh, to be in England
Now that April's there,
And whoever wakes in England
Sees, some morning, unaware,
That the lowest boughs and brushwood sheaf
Round the elm-tree bole are in tiny leaf,
While the chaffinch sings on the orchard bough
In England – now!

II

And after April, when May follows,
And the whitethroat builds, and all the swallows!
Hark, where my blossomed pear-tree in the hedge
Leans to the field and scatters on the clover
Blossoms and dewdrops – at the bent spray's edge –
That's the wise thrush; he sings each song twice over,
Lest you should think he never could recapture
The first fine careless rapture!
And though the fields look rough with hoary dew
All will be gay when noontide wakes anew
The buttercups, the little children's dower
– Far brighter than this gaudy melon-flower!

Robert Browning (1812–1889)

2ND APRIL

Ten Songs: V

Dog   The single creature leads a partial life,
       Man by his mind, and by his nose the hound;
       He needs the deep emotions I can give,
       I scent him in a vaster hunting ground.

Cats   Like calls to like, to share is to relieve
       And sympathy the root bears love the flower;
       He feels with us, and in him we perceive
       A common passion for the lonely hour.

Cats   We move in our apartness and our pride
       About the decent dwellings he has made:
Dog   In all his walks I follow at his side,
       His faithful servant and his loving shade.

W. H. Auden (1907–1973)

3RD APRIL

The Woodspurge

The wind flapped loose, the wind was still,
Shaken out dead from tree and hill:
I had walked on at the wind's will, –
I sat now, for the wind was still.

Between my knees my forehead was, –
My lips, drawn in, said not Alas!
My hair was over in the grass,
My naked ears heard the day pass.

My eyes, wide open, had the run
Of some ten weeds to fix upon;
Among those few, out of the sun,
The woodspurge flowered, three cups in one.

From perfect grief there need not be
Wisdom or even memory:
One thing then learnt remains to me, –
The woodspurge has a cup of three.

D. G. Rossetti (1828–1882)

4TH APRIL

Scale Force, Cumberland

It sweeps, as sweeps an army
Adown the mountain-side,
With the voice of many thunders
Like the battle's sounding tide.

Yet the sky is blue above it,
And the dashing of the spray
Wears the colour of the rainbow
Upon an April day.

It rejoices in the sunshine
When after heavy rain
It gathers the far waters
To dash upon the plain.

It is terrible yet lovely
Beneath the morning rays,
Like a dream of strength and beauty
It haunted those who gaze.

We feel that it is glorious –
Its power is on the soul –
And lofty thoughts within us
Acknowledge its control.

A generous inspiration
Is on the outward world –
It waketh thoughts and feelings
In a careless coldness furled.

To love and to admire
Seems natural to the heart;
Life's small and selfish interests
From such a scene depart!

Letitia Elizabeth Landon (1802–1838)

5TH APRIL

April

LINES 1–13

'THE SPRING COMES SLOWLY UP THIS WAY.'

CHRISTABEL

'Tis the noon of the spring-time, yet never a bird
In the wind-shaken elm or the maple is heard;
For green meadow-grasses wide levels of snow,
And blowing of drifts where the crocus should
  blow;
Where wind-flower and violet, amber and white,
On south-sloping brooksides should smile in the
  light,
O'er the cold winter-beds of their late-waking
  roots
The frosty flake eddies, the ice-crystal shoots;
And, longing for light, under wind-driven heaps,
Round the boles of the pine-wood the ground-laurel
  creeps,
Unkissed of the sunshine, unbaptized of showers,
With buds scarcely swelled, which should burst
  into flowers!
We wait for thy coming, sweet wind of the south!

John Greenleaf Whittier (1807–1892)

6TH APRIL

Beachy Head

LINES 346–367

An early worshipper at nature's shrine,
I loved her rudest scenes – warrens, and heaths,
And yellow commons, and birch-shaded hollows,
And hedgerows, bordering unfrequented lanes,
Bowered with wild roses, and the clasping woodbine
Where purple tassels of the tangling vetch
With bittersweet, and bryony inweave,
And the dew fills the silver bindweed's cups –
I loved to trace the brooks whose humid banks
Nourish the harebell, and the freckled pagil;
And stroll among o'ershadowing woods of beech,
Lending in summer, from the heats of noon
A whispering shade; while haply there reclines
Some pensive lover of uncultured flowers,
Who, from the tumps with bright green mosses clad,
Plucks the wood-sorrel, with its light thin leaves,
Heart-shaped, and triply-folded; and its root
Creeping like beaded coral; or who there
Gathers, the copse's pride, anemones,
With rays like golden studs on ivory laid
Most delicate: but touched with purple clouds,
Fit crown for April's fair but changeful brow.

Charlotte Smith (1749–1806)

7TH APRIL

In a London Square

Put forth thy leaf, thou lofty plane,
   East wind and frost are safely gone;
With zephyr mild and balmy rain
   The summer comes serenely on;
Earth, air, and sun and skies combine
   To promise all that's kind and fair: –
But thou, O human heart of mine,
   Be still, contain thyself, and bear.

December days were brief and chill,
   The winds of March were wild and drear,
And, nearing and receding still,
   Spring never would, we thought, be here.
The leaves that burst, the suns that shine,
   Had, not the less, their certain date: –
And thou, O human heart of mine,
   Be still, refrain thyself, and wait.

Arthur Hugh Clough (1819–1861)

8TH APRIL

Night

night finds us, creeping soundlessly
past window pane, through door ajar:
and not even a candle's glow
can halt the irredeeming course.

the curtains drawn prevent the skulk
of dark's advance, but not too much:
the night expands and we accept
its scalding web, with no remorse.

Joel Knight (1975–)

9TH APRIL

The Crow

With rakish eye and plenished crop,
  Oblivious of the farmer's gun,
Upon the naked ash-tree top
  The Crow sits basking in the sun.

An old ungodly rogue, I wot!
  For, perched in black against the blue,
His feathers, torn with beak and shot,
  Let woeful glints of April through.

The year's new grass, and, golden-eyed,
  The daisies sparkle underneath,
And chestnut-trees on either side
  Have opened every ruddy sheath.

But doubtful still of frost and snow,
  The ash alone stands stark and bare,
And on its topmost twig the Crow
  Takes the glad morning's sun and air.

William Canton (1845–1926)

10ᵀᴴ APRIL

An April Day

Breezes strongly rushing, when the North-West
  stirs,
Prophesying Summer to the shaken firs;
Blowing brows of forest, where soft airs are free,
Crowned with heavenly glimpses of the shining
  sea;
Buds and breaking blossoms, that sunny April
  yields;
Ferns and fairy grasses, the children of the fields;
In the fragrant hedges' hollow brambled gloom
Pure primroses paling into perfect bloom;
Round the elms rough stature, climbing dark and
  high,
Ivy-fringes trembling against a golden sky;
Woods and windy ridges darkening in the glow;
The rosy sunset bathing all the vale below;
Violet banks forsaken in the fading light;
Starry sadness filling the quiet eyes of night;
Dew on all things drooping for the summer rains;
Dewy daisies folding in the lonely lanes.

Laurence Binyon (1869–1943)

11TH APRIL

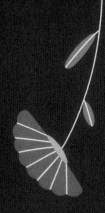

The Birds and the Flowers

FROM *MILTON*, BOOK 2, PLATE 31, LINES 28–45

Thou hearest the Nightingale begin the Song of
  Spring:
The Lark, sitting upon his earthy bed, just as the
  morn
Appears, listens silent; then, springing from the
  waving corn-field, loud
He leads the Choir of Day – trill! trill! trill! trill!
Mounting upon the wings of light into the great
  Expanse,
Re-echoing against the lovely blue and shining
  heavenly Shell;
His little throat labours with inspiration; every
  feather
On throat and breast and wings vibrates with the
  effluence Divine.
All Nature listens to him silent, and the awful Sun
Stands still upon the mountains, looking on this
  little Bird

With eyes of soft humility and wonder, love and
   awe.
Then loud, from their green covert, all the Birds
   begin their song:
The Thrush, the Linnet and the Goldfinch, Robin
   and the Wren,
Awake the Sun from his sweet reverie upon the
   mountain:
The Nightingale again essays his song, and thro'
   the day
And thro' the night warbles luxuriant; every Bird
   of song
Attending his loud harmony with admiration
   and love.
This is a Vision of the lamentation of Beulah
   over Ololon.

William Blake (1757–1827)

12TH APRIL

Afton Water

Flow gently, sweet Afton, among thy green braes,
Flow gently, I'll sing thee a song in thy praise;
My Mary's asleep by thy murmuring stream,
Flow gently, sweet Afton, disturb not her dream.

Thou stock-dove, whose echo resounds thro' the glen,
Ye wild whistling blackbirds in yon thorny den,
Thou green-crested lapwing, thy screaming forbear,
I charge you disturb not my slumbering fair.

How lofty, sweet Afton, thy neighbouring hills,
Far mark'd with the courses of clear winding rills;
There daily I wander as noon rises high,
My flocks and my Mary's sweet cot in my eye.

How pleasant thy banks and green valleys below,
Where wild in the woodlands the primroses blow;
There oft, as mild ev'ning sweeps over the lea,
The sweet-scented birk shades my Mary and me.

Thy crystal stream, Afton, how lovely it glides,
And winds by the cot where my Mary resides,
How wanton thy waters her snowy feet lave,
As gathering sweet flowrets she stems thy clear wave.

Flow gently, sweet Afton, among thy green braes,
Flow gently, sweet river, the theme of my lays;
My Mary's asleep by thy murmuring stream,
Flow gently, sweet Afton, disturb not her dream.

Robert Burns (1759–1796)

13TH APRIL

Buds

The raining hour is done,
    And, threaded on the bough,
The may-buds in the sun
    Are shining emeralds now.

As transitory these
    As things of April will,
Yet, trembling in the trees,
    Is briefer beauty still.

For, flowering from the sky
    Upon an April day,
Are silver buds that lie
    Amid the buds of may.

The April emeralds now,
    While thrushes fill the lane,
Are linked along the bough
    With silver buds of rain.

And, straightly though to earth
    The buds of silver slip,
The green buds keep the mirth
    Of that companionship.

John Drinkwater (1882–1937)

14TH APRIL

Repeat That, Repeat

Repeat that, repeat,
Cuckoo, bird, and open ear wells, heart-springs,
 delightfully sweet,
With a ballad, with a ballad, a rebound
Off trundled timber and scoops of the hillside
 ground, hollow hollow hollow ground:
The whole landscape flushes on a sudden at a sound.

Gerard Manley Hopkins (1844–1889)

15TH APRIL

April

A bird chirped at my window this morning,
And over the sky is drawn a light network of clouds.
Come,
Let us go out into the open,
For my heart leaps like a fish that is ready to spawn.

I will lie under the beech-trees,
Under the grey branches of the beech-trees,
In a blueness of little squills and crocuses.
I will lie among the little squills
And be delivered of this overcharge of beauty,
And that which is born shall be a joy to you
Who love me.

Amy Lowell (1874–1925)

16TH APRIL

Bird Raptures

The sunrise wakes the lark to sing,
  The moonrise wakes the nightingale.
Come darkness, moonrise, everything
  That is so silent, sweet, and pale,
  Come, so ye wake the nightingale.

Make haste to mount, thou wistful moon,
  Make haste to wake the nightingale:
Let silence set the world in tune
  To hearken to that wordless tale
  Which warbles from the nightingale.

O herald skylark, stay thy flight
  One moment, for a nightingale
Floods us with sorrow and delight.
  To-morrow thou shalt hoist the sail;
  Leave us tonight the nightingale.

Christina Rossetti (1830–1894)

17ᵀᴴ APRIL

I Wandered Lonely as a Cloud

WRITTEN AT TOWN-END, GRASMERE.

I wandered lonely as a cloud
That floats on high o'er vales and hills,
When all at once I saw a crowd,
A host, of golden daffodils;
Beside the lake, beneath the trees,
Fluttering and dancing in the breeze.

Continuous as the stars that shine
And twinkle on the milky way,
They stretched in never-ending line
Along the margin of the bay:
Ten thousand saw I at a glance,
Tossing their heads in sprightly dance.

The waves beside them danced; but they
Out-did the sparkling waves in glee:
A poet could not but be gay,
In such a jocund company:
I gazed – and gazed – but little thought
What wealth the show to me had brought:

For oft, when on my couch I lie
In vacant or in pensive mood,
They flash upon that inward eye
Which is the bliss of solitude;
And then my heart with pleasure fills,
And dances with the daffodils.

William Wordsworth (1770–1850)

18TH APRIL

The Loveliest of Trees

A SHROPSHIRE LAD, II

Loveliest of trees, the cherry now
Is hung with bloom along the bough,
And stands about the woodlands ride
Wearing white for Eastertide.

Now, of my threescore years and ten,
Twenty will not come again,
And take from seventy springs a score,
It only leaves me fifty more.

And since to look at things in bloom
Fifty springs are little room,
About the woodlands I will go
To see the cherry hung with snow.

A. E. Housman (1859–1936)

19TH APRIL

Quail's Nest

I wandered out one rainy day
And heard a bird with merry joys
Cry 'wet my foot' for half the way
I stood and wondered at the noise

When from my foot a bird did flee
The rain flew bouncing from her breast
I wondered what the bird could be
And almost trampled on her nest

The nest was full of eggs and round
I met a shepherd in the vales
And stood to tell him what I found.
He knew and said it was a quails

For he himself the nest had found
Among the wheat and on the green
When going on his daily round
With eggs as many as fifteen

Among the stranger birds they feed
Their summer flight is short and low
Theres very few know where they breed
And scarcely any where they go

John Clare (1793–1864)

20TH APRIL

A Flower of the Himalayas

A flower of the Himalayas
on this Welsh hillside, says its prayers.
A flower from another land
is trying to make us understand.
Its prayers, though they be Hindu
are yet the same,
for me and you.

David Austin (1926–2018)

21ST APRIL

Apple Blossoms

Amid the young year's breathing hopes,
  When eager grasses wrap the earth,
I see on greening orchard slopes
  The blossoms trembling into birth.
They open wide their rosy palms
  To feel the hesitating rain,
Or beg a longed-for golden alms
  From skies that deep in clouds have lain.

They mingle with the bluebird's songs,
  And with the warm wind's reverie;
To sward and stream their snow belongs,
  To neighboring pines in flocks they flee,
O doubly crowned with breathing hopes
  The branches bending down to earth
That feel on greening orchard slopes
  Their blossoms trembling into birth!

Ethelwyn Wetherald (1857–1940)

22ND APRIL

Thyrsis

A MONODY, TO COMMEMORATE THE AUTHOR'S FRIEND,
ARTHUR HUGH CLOUGH, WHO DIED AT FLORENCE, 1861
VERSE 12

I know these slopes; who knows them if not I? –
But many a dingle on the loved hill-side,
With thorns once studded, old, white-blossom'd
trees,
Where thick the cowslips grew, and far descried
High tower'd the spikes of purple orchises,
Hath since our day put by
The coronals of that forgotten time;
Down each green bank hath gone the
ploughboy's team,
And only in the hidden brookside gleam
Primroses, orphans of the flowery prime.

Matthew Arnold (1822–1888)

23ᴿᴰ APRIL

Hark, Hark, the Lark

FROM *CYMBELINE*, ACT II, SCENE III

Hark, hark, the lark at heaven gate sings,
   And Phoebus gins arise,
His steeds to water at those springs
   On chaliced flowers that lies,
And winking Mary-buds begin to ope their
                   golden eyes;
With everything that pretty is, my lady sweet, arise,
   Arise, arise!

William Shakespeare (1564–1616)

24TH APRIL

The Nightingale

A CONVERSATION POEM, APRIL, 1798

LINES 1–39

No cloud, no relique of the sunken day
Distinguishes the West, no long thin slip
Of sullen light, no obscure trembling hues.
Come, we will rest on this old mossy bridge!
You see the glimmer of the stream beneath,
But hear no murmuring: it flows silently.
O'er its soft bed of verdure. All is still.
A balmy night! and though the stars be dim,
Yet let us think upon the vernal showers
That gladden the green earth, and we shall find
A pleasure in the dimness of the stars.
And hark! the Nightingale begins its song,
'Most musical, most melancholy' bird!
A melancholy bird? Oh! idle thought!
In Nature there is nothing melancholy.
But some night-wandering man whose heart was
    pierced
With the remembrance of a grievous wrong,
Or slow distemper, or neglected love,
(And so, poor wretch! filled all things with himself,
And made all gentle sounds tell back the tale

Of his own sorrow) he, and such as he,
First named these notes a melancholy strain.
And many a poet echoes the conceit;
Poet who hath been building up the rhyme
When he had better far have stretched his limbs
Beside a brook in mossy forest-dell,
By sun or moon-light, to the influxes
Of shapes and sounds and shifting elements
Surrendering his whole spirit, of his song
And of his fame forgetful! so his fame
Should share in Nature's immortality,
A venerable thing! and so his song
Should make all Nature lovelier, and itself
Be loved like Nature! But 'twill not be so;
And youths and maidens most poetical,
Who lose the deepening twilights of the spring
In ball-rooms and hot theatres, they still
Full of meek sympathy must heave their sighs
O'er Philomela's pity-pleading strains.

Samuel Taylor Coleridge (1772–1834)

25TH APRIL

April's Charms

When April scatters coins of primrose gold
Among the copper leaves in thickets old,
And singing skylarks from the meadows rise,
To twinkle like black stars in sunny skies;

When I can hear the small woodpecker ring
Time on a tree for all the birds that sing;
And hear the pleasant cuckoo, loud and long –
The simple bird that thinks two notes a song;

When I can hear the woodland brook, that could
Not drown a babe, with all his threatening mood;
Upon these banks the violets make their home,
And let a few small strawberry blossoms come:

When I go forth on such a pleasant day,
One breath outdoors takes all my cares away;
It goes like heavy smoke, when flames take hold
Of wood that's green and fill a grate with gold.

W. H. Davies (1871–1940)

26TH APRIL

Bluebells

Like smoke held down by frost
The bluebells wreathe in the wood.
Spring like a swan there
Feeds on a cold flood:

But the winter woodmen know
How to make flame
From sodden December faggots,
They can make the blue smoke climb.

Picked flowers wilt at once,
They flare but where they are;
The swan will not sing nor the fire thrive
In a town-watered jar:

But the winter woodmen know
The essential secret burning;
The fire at the earth's core
In touch with the turning sun.

Patric Dickinson (1914–1994)

27ᵀᴴ APRIL

The Shepheardes Calender, Aprill

LINES 136–144

Bring hether the Pincke and purple Cullambine,
　With Gelliflowres:
Bring Coronations, and Sops in wine,
　Worne of Paramoures.
Strowe me the ground with Daffadowndillies,
And Cowslips, and Kingcups, and loved Lillies:
　The pretie Pawnce,
　And the Cheuisaunce,
Shall match with the fayre flowre Delice.

Edmund Spenser (c.1552–1599)

28TH APRIL

March Strongly Forth

FROM *POLY-OLBION*, SONG II, LINES 1–18

March strongly forth, my Muse, whilst yet the
  temperate air
Invites us easily on to hasten our repair.
Thou powerful god of flames (in verse divinely great)
Touch my invention so with thy true genuine heat
That high and noble things I slightly may not tell,
Nor light and idle toys my lines may vainly swell;
But, as my subject serves, so high or low to strain,
And to the varying earth so suit my varying vein,
That, nature, in my work thou mayst thy power avow;
That, as thou first foundst art and didst her rules
  allow,
So I, to thine own self that gladly near would be,
May herein do the best, in imitating thee.
As thou hast here a hill, a vale there, there a flood,
A mead here, there a heath, and now and then a
  wood,
These things so in my song I naturally may show:
Now as the mountain high, then as the valley low;
Here fruitful as the mead, there as the heath be bare;
Then, as the gloomy wood, I may be rough, though
  rare.

Michael Drayton (1563–1631)

29TH APRIL

Parta Quies

Good-night; ensured release,
Imperishable peace,
    Have these for yours,
While sea abides, and land,
And earth's foundations stand,
    And heaven endures.

When earth's foundations flee,
Nor sky nor land nor sea
    At all is found,
Content you, let them burn:
It is not your concern;
    Sleep on, sleep sound.

A. E. Housman (1859–1936)

30TH APRIL

The April Sky Sags Low and Drear

PRAELUDIUM, VII

The April sky sags low and drear,
  The April winds blow cold,
The April rains fall gray and sheer,
  And yeanlings keep the fold.

But the rook has built, and the song-birds quire,
  And over the faded lea
The lark soars glorying, gyre on gyre,
  And he is the bird for me!

For he sings as if from his watchman's height
  He saw, this blighting day,
The far vales break into colour and light
  From the banners and arms of May.

W. E. Henley (1849–1903)

MAY

The Moon Shines White and Silent

1ST MAY

Night of Frost in May

LINES 1–14

With splendour of a silver day,
A frosted night had opened May:
And on that plumed and armoured night,
As one close temple hove our wood,
Its border leafage virgin white.
Remote down air an owl hallooed.
The black twig dropped without a twirl;
The bud in jewelled grasp was nipped;
The brown leaf cracked a scorching curl;
A crystal off the green leaf slipped.
Across the tracks of rimy tan,
Some busy thread at whiles would shoot;
A limping minnow-rillet ran,
To hang upon an icy foot.

George Meredith (1828–1909)

2ND MAY

By Severn

If England, her spirit lives anywhere
It is by Severn, by hawthorns and grand willows.
Earth heaves up twice a hundred feet in air
And ruddy clay falls scooped out to the weedy shallows.
There in the brakes of May Spring has her chambers,
Robing-rooms of hawthorn, cowslip, cuckoo flower –
Wonder complete changes for each square joy's hour,
Past thought miracles are there and beyond numbers.
If for the drab atmospheres and managed lighting
In London town, Oriana's playwrights had
Wainlode her theatre and then coppice clad
Hill for her ground of sauntering and idle waiting,
Why, then I think, our chiefest glory of pride
(The Elizabethans of Thames, South and Northern side)
Would nothing of its needing be denied,
And her sons praises from England's mouth again be
   outcried.

Ivor Gurney (1890–1937)

3RD MAY

Sonnet

After dark vapors have oppress'd our plains
   For a long dreary season, comes a day
   Born of the gentle South, and clears away
From the sick heavens all unseemly stains.
The anxious month, relieved of its pains,
   Takes as a long-lost right the feel of May;
   The eyelids with the passing coolness play
Like rose leaves with the drip of Summer rains.
The calmest thoughts came round us; as of leaves
Budding – fruit ripening in stillness – Autumn suns
   Smiling at eve upon the quiet sheaves –
Sweet Sappho's cheek – a smiling infant's breath –
   The gradual sand that through an hour-glass runs –
A woodland rivulet – a Poet's death.

John Keats (1795–1821)

4TH MAY

The Trees

The trees are coming into leaf
Like something almost being said;
The recent buds relax and spread,
Their greenness is a kind of grief.

Is it that they are born again
And we grow old? No, they die too,
Their yearly trick of looking new
Is written down in rings of grain.

Yet still the unresting castles thresh
In fullgrown thickness every May.
Last year is dead, they seem to say,
Begin afresh, afresh, afresh.

Philip Larkin (1922–1985)

5TH MAY

Voices of the Night

Pleasant it was, when woods were green
  And winds were soft and low,
To lie amid some sylvan scene,
Where, the long drooping boughs between,
Shadows dark and sunlight sheen
  Alternate come and go;

Or where the denser grove receives
  No sunlight from above,
But the dark foliage interweaves
In one unbroken roof of leaves,
Underneath whose sloping eaves
  The shadows hardly move.

Beneath some patriarchal tree
  I lay upon the ground;
His hoary arms uplifted he,
And all the broad leaves over me
Clapped their little hands in glee,
  With one continuous sound; –

A slumberous sound, a sound that brings
  The feelings of a dream,
As of innumerable wings,
As, when a bell no longer swings,
Faint the hollow murmur rings
  O'er meadow, lake, and stream.

Henry Wadsworth Longfellow (1807–1882)

6TH MAY

Midnight

The moon shines white and silent
  On the mist, which, like a tide
Of some enchanted ocean,
  O'er the wide marsh doth glide,
Spreading its ghost-like billows
  Silently far and wide.

A vague and starry magic
  Makes all things mysteries,
And lures the earth's dumb spirit
  Up to the longing skies, –
I seem to hear dim whispers,
  And tremulous replies.

The fireflies o'er the meadow
  In pulses come and go;
The elm-trees' heavy shadow
  Weighs on the grass below;
And faintly from the distance
  The dreaming cock doth crow.

All things look strange and mystic,
  The very bushes swell
And take wild shapes and motions,
  As if beneath a spell;
They seem not the same lilacs
  From childhood known so well.

The snow of deepest silence
  O'er everything doth fall,
So beautiful and quiet,
  And yet so like a pall;
As if all life were ended,
  And rest were come to all.

O wild and wondrous midnight,
  There is a might in thee
To make the charmèd body
  Almost like spirit be,
And give it some faint glimpses
  Of immortality!

James Russell Lowell (1819–1891)

7TH MAY

The Mystery

If sunset clouds could grow on trees
It would but match the may in flower;
And skies be underneath the seas
No topsyturvier than a shower.

If mountains rose on wings to wander
They were no wilder than a cloud;
Yet all my praise is mean as slander,
Mean as these mean words spoken aloud.

And never more than now I know
That man's first heaven is far behind;
Unless the blazing seraph's blow
Has left him in the garden blind.

Witness, O Sun that blinds our eyes,
Unthinkable and unthankable King,
That though all other wonder dies
I wonder at not wondering.

G. K. Chesterton (1874–1936)

8TH MAY

The Lilac is in Bloom

FROM *THE OLD VICARAGE, GRANTCHESTER*

(CAFÉ DES WESTENS, BERLIN, MAY 1912)

Just now the lilac is in bloom,
All before my little room;
And in my flower-beds, I think,
Smile the carnations and the pink;
And down the borders, well I know,
The poppy and the pansy blow ...
Oh! there the chestnuts, summer through,
Beside the river make for you
A tunnel of green gloom, and sleep
Deeply above; and green and deep
The stream mysterious glides beneath,
Green as a dream and deep as death.
– Oh, damn! I know it! and I know
How the May fields all golden show,
And when the day is young and sweet,
Gild gloriously the bare feet
That run to bathe ...

Ah God! to see the branches stir
Across the moon at Grantchester!
To smell the thrilling-sweet and rotten
Unforgettable, unforgotten

River-smell, and hear the breeze
Sobbing in the little trees.
Say, do the elm-clumps greatly stand
Still guardians of that holy land?
The chestnuts shade, in reverend dream,
The yet unacademic stream?
Is dawn a secret shy and cold
Anadyomene, silver and gold?
And sunset still a golden sea
From Haslingfield to Madingley?
And after, ere the night is born,
Do hares come out about the corn?
Oh, is the water sweet and cool,
Gentle and brown, above the pool?
And laughs the immortal river still
Under the mill, under the mill?
Say, is there Beauty yet to find?
And Certainty? and Quiet kind?
Deep meadows yet, for to forget
The lies, and truths, and pain? ... oh! yet
Stands the Church clock at ten to three?
And is there honey still for tea?

Rupert Brooke (1887–1915)

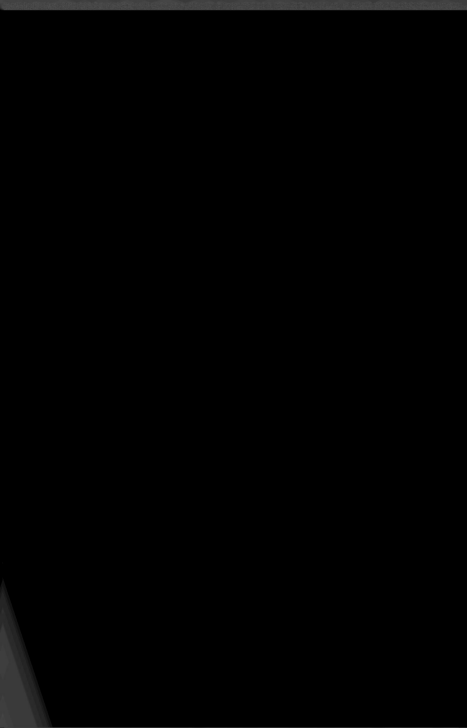

The Green Linnet

Beneath these fruit-tree boughs that shed
Their snow-white blossoms on my head,
With brightest sunshine round me spread
  Of spring's unclouded weather,
In this sequestered nook how sweet
To sit upon my orchard-seat!
And birds and flowers once more to greet,
  My last year's friends together.

One have I marked, the happiest guest
In all this covert of the blest:
Hail to Thee, far above the rest
  In joy of voice and pinion!
Thou, Linnet! in thy green array,
Presiding Spirit here to-day,
Dost lead the revels of the May;
  And this is thy dominion.

While birds, and butterflies, and flowers,
Make all one band of paramours,
Thou, ranging up and down the bowers,
  Art sole in thy employment:
A Life, a Presence like the Air,

Scattering thy gladness without care,
Too blest with any one to pair;
  Thyself thy own enjoyment.

Amid yon tuft of hazel trees,
That twinkle to the gusty breeze,
Behold him perched in ecstasies,
  Yet seeming still to hover;
There! where the flutter of his wings
Upon his back and body flings
Shadows and sunny glimmerings,
  That cover him all over.

My dazzled sight he oft deceives,
A brother of the dancing leaves;
Then flits, and from the cottage-eaves
  Pours forth his song in gushes;
As if by that exulting strain
He mocked and treated with disdain
The voiceless Form he chose to feign,
While fluttering in the bushes.

William Wordsworth (1770–1850)

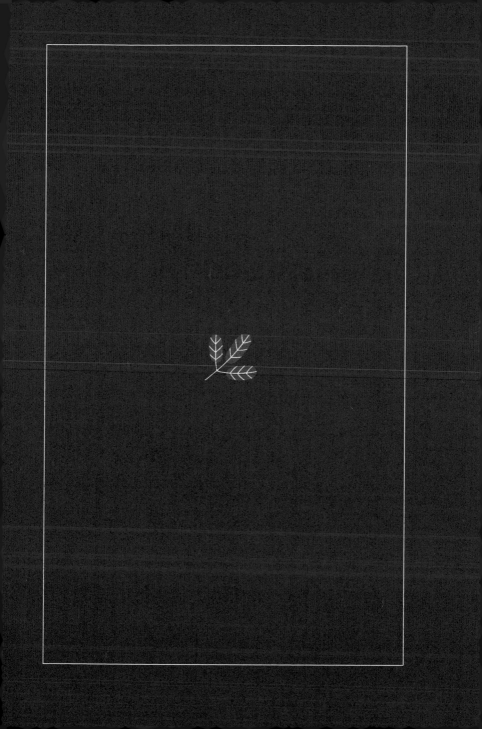

10TH MAY

The Vision of Piers Plowman

PROLOGUE, LINES 1–10

In a somer sesun whan soft was the sonne,
I shope me in shroudes as I a shepe were;
In habite as an heremite unholy of workes
Went wyde in this world wondres to here.
Ac on a May mornynge on Malverne hulles
Me byfel a ferly of fairy, me thoughte;
I was wery forwandred and went me to reste
Undur a brod banke bi a bornes side,
And as I lay and lened and loked in the watres,
I slombred in a slepyng it sweyued so merye.

William Langland (c.1332–c.1400)

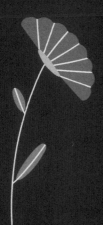

11TH MAY

The First Dandelion

Simple and fresh and fair from winter's close
    emerging,
As if no artifice of fashion, business, politics, had
    ever been,
Forth from its sunny nook of shelter'd grass –
    innocent, golden, calm as the dawn,
The spring's first dandelion shows its trustful face.

Walt Whitman (1819–1892)

12TH MAY

Ode to a Nightingale

VERSES I–IV

I

My heart aches, and a drowsy numbness pains
　　My sense, as though of hemlock I had drunk,
Or emptied some dull opiate to the drains
　　One minute past, and Lethe-wards had sunk:
'Tis not through envy of thy happy lot,
　　But being too happy in thine happiness, –
　　　　That thou, light-winged Dryad of the trees,
　　　　　　In some melodious plot
　　Of beechen green, and shadows numberless,
Singest of summer in full-throated ease.

II

O, for a draught of vintage! that hath been
　　Cool'd a long age in the deep-delved earth,
Tasting of Flora and the country green,
　　Dance, and Provençal song, and sunburnt mirth!
O for a beaker full of the warm South,
　　Full of the true, the blushful Hippocrene,
　　　　With beaded bubbles winking at the brim,
　　　　　　And purple-stained mouth;
　　That I might drink, and leave the world unseen,
　　And with thee fade away into the forest dim:

II

Fade far away, dissolve, and quite forget
  What thou among the leaves hast never known,
The weariness, the fever, and the fret
  Here, where men sit and hear each other groan;
Where palsy shakes a few, sad, last grey hairs,
  Where youth grows pale, and spectre-thin, and dies;
    Where but to think is to be full of sorrow
     And leaden-eyed despairs,
Where Beauty cannot keep her lustrous eyes,
  Or new Love pine at them beyond to-morrow.

IV

Away! away! for I will fly to thee,
  Not charioted by Bacchus and his pards,
But on the viewless wings of Poesy,
  Though the dull brain perplexes and retards:
Already with thee! tender is the night,
  And haply the Queen-Moon is on her throne,
    Cluster'd around by all her starry Fays;
     But here there is no light,
Save what from heaven is with the breezes blown
  Through verdurous glooms and winding mossy ways.

John Keats (1795–1821)

13ᵀᴴ MAY

A Brilliant Day

O keen pellucid air! nothing can lurk
Or disavow itself on this bright day;
The small rain-plashes shine from far away,
The tiny emmet glitters at his work;
The bee looks blithe and gay, and as she plies
Her task, and moves and sidles round the cup
Of this spring flower, to drink its honey up,
Her glassy wings, like oars that dip and rise,
Gleam momently. Pure-bosomed, clear of fog,
The long lake glistens, while the glorious beam
Bespangles the wet joints and floating leaves
Of water-plants, whose every point receives
His light; and jellies of the spawning frog,
Unmarked before, like piles of jewels seem!

Charles Tennyson Turner (1808–1879)

14TH MAY

Nightingales

Beautiful must be the mountains whence ye come,
And bright in the fruitful valleys the streams, wherefrom
    Ye learn your song:
Where are those starry woods? O might I
        wander there,
  Among the flowers, which in that heavenly air
    Bloom the year long!

Nay, barren are those mountains and spent the streams:
Our song is the voice of desire, that haunts our dreams,
    A throe of the heart,
Whose pining visions dim, forbidden hopes profound,
  No dying cadence, nor long sigh can sound,
    For all our art.

Alone, aloud in the raptured ear of men
We pour our dark nocturnal secret; and then,
    As night is withdrawn
From these sweet-springing meads and bursting
        boughs of May,
  Dream, while the innumerable choir of day
    Welcome the dawn.

Robert Bridges (1844–1930)

15TH MAY

Hedges

'Bread and cheese' grow wild in the green time,
   Children laugh and pick it, and I make my rhyme
For mere pleasure of seeing that so subtle play,
   Of arms and various legs going every, any, other
                 way.

And they turn and laugh for the unexpensiveness
   Of country grocery and are pleased no less
Than hedge sparrows. Lessons will be easier taken,
   For this gypsy chaffering, the hedge plucked and
                green shaken.

Ivor Gurney (1890–1937)

16TH MAY

The Lily of the Valley

Some flowers there are that rear their heads on high,
The gorgeous products of a burning sky,
That rush upon the eye with garish bloom,
And make the senses drunk with high perfume.
Not such art thou, sweet Lily of the Vale!
So lovely, small, and delicately pale, –
We might believe, if such fond faith were ours,
As sees humanity in trees and flowers,
That thou wert once a maiden, meek and good,
That pined away beneath her native wood
For very fear of her own loveliness,
And died of love she never would confess.

Hartley Coleridge (1796–1849)

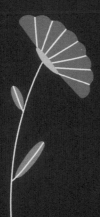

17TH MAY

Ode on the Spring

Lo! where the rosy-bosom'd Hours,
    Fair Venus' train appear,
Disclose the long-expecting flowers,
    And wake the purple year!
The Attic warbler pours her throat,
Responsive to the cuckoo's note,
    The untaught harmony of spring:
While, whisp'ring pleasure as they fly,
Cool Zephyrs thro' the clear blue sky
    Their gather'd fragrance fling.

Where'er the oak's thick branches stretch
    A broader browner shade;
Where'er the rude and moss-grown beech
    O'er-canopies the glade,
Beside some water's rushy brink
With me the Muse shall sit, and think
    (At ease reclin'd in rustic state)
How vain the ardour of the crowd,
How low, how little are the proud,
    How indigent the great!

Still is the toiling hand of Care;
   The panting herds repose:
Yet hark, how thro' the peopled air
   The busy murmur glows!
The insect-youth are on the wing,
Eager to taste the honied spring,
   And float amid the liquid noon:
Some lightly o'er the current skim,
Some show their gayly-gilded trim
   Quick-glancing to the sun.

Thomas Gray (1716–1771)

18ᵀᴴ MAY

Golden Glories

The buttercup is like a golden cup,
   The marigold is like a golden frill,
The daisy with a golden eye looks up,
   And golden spreads the flag beside the rill,
   And gay and golden nods the daffodil,
The gorsey common swells a golden sea,
   The cowslip hangs a head of golden tips,
And golden drips the honey which the bee
   Sucks from sweet hearts of flowers and stores
                    and sips.

Christina Rossetti (1830–1894)

19TH MAY

Sonnet

O nightingale, that on yon bloomy spray
  Warblest at eve, when all the woods are still,
  Thou with fresh hope the lover's heart dost fill,
  While the jolly hours lead on propitious May,
Thy liquid notes that close the eye of day,
  First heard before the shallow cuckoo's bill
  Portend success in love. O, if Jove's will
  Have linked that amorous power to thy soft lay,
Now timely sing, ere the rude bird of hate
  Foretell my hopeless doom in some grove nigh,
  As thou from year to year hast sung too late
For my relief, yet hadst no reason why,
  Whether the Muse or Love call thee his mate
  Both them I serve, and of their train am I.

John Milton (1608–1674)

20TH MAY

May, 1915

Let us remember Spring will come again
To the scorched, blackened woods, where the
                    wounded trees
Wait, with their old wise patience for the
                    heavenly rain,
Sure of the sky: sure of the sea to send its healing
                    breeze,
        Sure of the sun. And even as to these
            Surely the Spring, when God shall please,
        Will come again like a divine surprise
To those who sit to-day with their great Dead,
                    hands in their hands, eyes
                        in their eyes,
At one with Love, at one with Grief:
                    blind to the scattered things
                    and changing skies.

Charlotte Mew (1869–1928)

21ST MAY

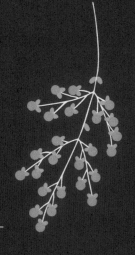

A Nocturnal Reverie

LINES 1–18

In such a night, when every louder wind
Is to its distant cavern safe confined;
And only gentle Zephyr fans his wings,
And lonely Philomel, still waking, sings;
Or from some tree, famed for the owl's delight,
She, hollowing clear, directs the wanderer right:
In such a night, when passing clouds give place,
Or thinly veil the heavens' mysterious face;
When in some river, overhung with green,
The waving moon and the trembling leaves are seen;
When freshened grass now bears itself upright,
And makes cool banks to pleasing rest invite,
Whence springs the woodbind, and the bramble-rose,
And where the sleepy cowslip sheltered grows;
Whilst now a paler hue the foxglove takes,
Yet checkers still with red the dusky brakes
When scattered glow-worms, but in twilight fine,
Show trivial beauties, watch their hour to shine;

Anne Finch, Countess of Winchelsea (1661–1720)

22ND MAY

The Enviable Isles

FROM 'RAMMON'

Through storms you reach them and from storms
are free.
Afar descried, the foremost drear in hue,
But, nearer, green; and, on the marge, the sea
Makes thunder low and mist of rainbowed dew.

But, inland, where the sleep that folds the hills
A dreamier sleep, the trance of God, instills –
On uplands hazed, in wandering airs aswoon,
Slow-swaying palms salute love's cypress tree
Adown in vale where pebbly runlets croon
A song to lull all sorrow and all glee.

Sweet-fern and moss in many a glade are here.
Where, strewn in flocks, what cheek-flushed
myriads lie
Dimpling in dream – unconscious slumberers mere,
While billows endless round the beaches die.

Herman Melville (1819–1891)

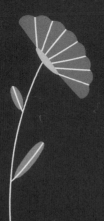

23ʳᵈ MAY

The Legend of Good Women

PROLOGUE, LINES 40–50

Now have I therto this condicioun
That, of alle the floures in the mede,
Than love I most these floures whyte and rede,
Swiche as men callen daysies in our toun.
To hem have I so greet affeccioun,
As I seyde erst, whan comen is the May,
That in my bed ther daweth me no day
That I nam up, and walking in the mede
To seen these floures agein the sonne sprede,
Whan it up-riseth by the morwe shene,
The longe day, thus walking in the grene.

Geoffrey Chaucer (c.1343–1400)

24TH MAY

The Vixen

Among the taller wood with ivy hung
The old fox plays and dances round her young
She snuffs and barks if any passes bye
And swings her tail and turns prepared to flye
The horseman hurries bye she bolts to see
And turns agen from danger never free
If any stands she runs among the poles
And barks and snaps and drive them in the holes
The shepherd sees them and the boy goes bye
And gets a stick and progs the hole to try
They get all still and lie in safty sure
And out again when safety is secure
And start and snap at blackbirds bouncing by
To fight and catch the great white butterflye

John Clare (1793–1864)

25TH MAY

Proportion

In the sky there is a moon and stars
And in my garden there are yellow moths
Fluttering about a white azalea bush.

Amy Lowell (1874–1925)

26TH MAY

Sedge-warblers

This beauty made me dream there was a time
Long past and irrecoverable, a clime
Where any brook so radiant racing clear
Through buttercup and kingcup bright as brass
But gentle, nourishing the meadow grass
That leans and scurries in the wind, would bear
Another beauty, divine and feminine,
Child to the sun, a nymph whose soul unstained
Could love all day, and never hate or tire,
A lover of mortal or immortal kin.

And yet, rid of this dream, ere I had drained
Its poison, quieted was my desire
So that I only looked into the water,
Clearer than any goddess or man's daughter,
And hearkened while it combed the dark green hair
And shook the millions of the blossoms white
Of water-crowfoot, and curdled to one sheet
The flowers fallen from the chestnuts in the park
Far off. And sedge-warblers, clinging so light

To willow twigs, sang longer than the lark,
Quick, shrill, or grating, a song to match the heat
Of the strong sun, nor less the water's cool,
Gushing through narrows, swirling in the pool.
Their song that lacks all words, all melody,
All sweetness almost, was dearer then to me
Than sweetest voice that sings in tune sweet words.
This was the best of May – the small brown birds
Wisely reiterating endlessly
What no man learnt yet, in or out of school.

Edward Thomas (1878–1917)

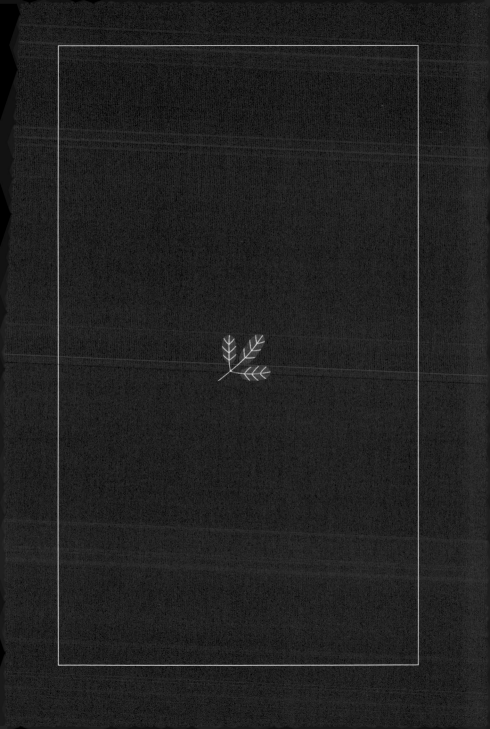

27TH MAY

O Were my Love Yon Lilac Fair

O were my love yon lilac fair,
  Wi' purple blossoms to the spring,
And I, a bird to shelter there,
  When wearied on my little wing;

How I wad mourn when it was torn
  By autumn wild, and winter rude!
But I wad sing on wanton wing,
  When youthfu' May its bloom renew'd.

O gin my love were yon red rose,
  That grows upon the castle wa',
And I mysel' a drap o' dew,
  Into her bonie breast to fa'!

Oh, there beyond expression blest,
  I'd feast on beauty a' the night;
Seal'd on her silk-saft faulds to rest,
  Till fley'd awa' by Phoebus' light.

Robert Burns (1759–1796)

28TH MAY

May Evening

So late the rustling shower was heard;
Yet now the aëry west is still.
The wet leaves flash, and lightly stirred
Great drops out of the lilac spill.
Peacefully blown, the ashen clouds
Uncurtain height on height of sky.
Here, as I wander, beauty crowds
In freshness keen upon my eye.

Now the shorn turf a glowing green
Takes in the massy cedar shade;
And through the poplar's trembling screen
Fires of the evening blush and fade.
Each way my marvelling senses feel
Swift odour, light, and luminous hue
Of leaf and flower upon them steal:
The songs of birds pierce my heart through.

The tulip clear, like yellow flame,
Burns upward from the gloomy mould:
As though for passion forth they came,
Red hearts of peonies unfold:
And perfumes tender, sweet, intense
Enter me, delicate as a blade.
The lilac odour wounds my sense,
Of the rich rose I am afraid.

Laurence Binyon (1869–1943)

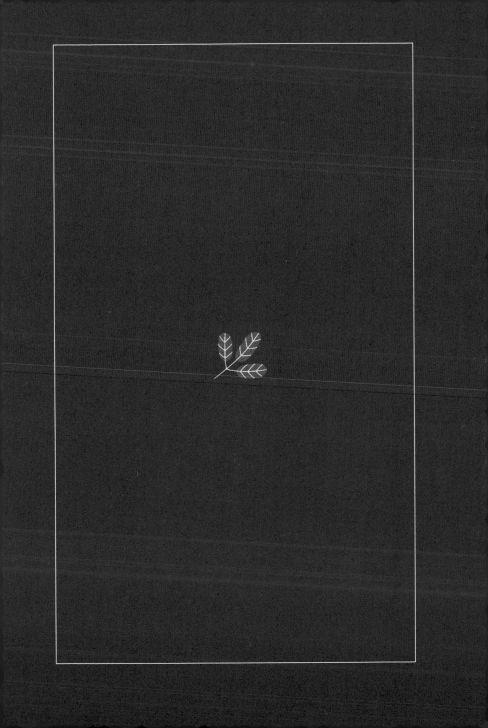

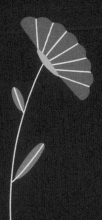

29TH MAY

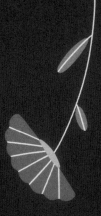

Of Many Worlds in This World

Just like unto a nest of boxes round,
Degrees of sizes within each box are found,
So, in this world, may many worlds more be,
Thinner, and less, and less still by degree;
Although they are not subject to our sense,
A world may be no bigger than twopence.
Nature is curious, and such work may make
That our dull sense can never find, but scape.
For creatures small as atoms may be there,
If every atom a creature's figure bear.
If four atoms a world can make, then see
What several worlds might in an ear-ring be.
For millions of those atoms may be in
The head of one small, little, single pin.
And if thus small, then ladies may well wear
A world of worlds as pendents in each ear.

Margaret Cavendish (1623–1673)

30TH MAY

In the Heart of the Forest

VERSES I–VIII

I

I heard the voice of my own true love
  Ripple the sunny weather.
Then away, as a dove that follows a dove,
  We flitted through woods together.

II

There was not a bush nor branch nor spray
  But with song was swaying and ringing.
'Let us ask of the birds what means their lay,
  And what is it prompts their singing.'

III

We paused where the stichwort and speedwell grew
  'Mid a forest of grasses fairy:
From out of the covert the cushat flew,
  And the squirrel perched shy and wary.

IV

On an elm-tree top shrilled a misselthrush proud,
  Disdaining shelter or screening.
'Now what is it makes you pipe so loud,
  And what is your music's meaning?

V

'Your matins begin ere the dewdrop sinks
   To the heart of the moist musk-roses,
And your vespers last till the first star winks,
   And the vigilant woodreeve dozes.'

VI

Then louder, still louder he shrilled: 'I sing
   For the pleasure and pride of shrilling,
For the sheen and the sap and the showers of Spring
   That fill me to overfilling.

VII

'Yet a something deeper than Spring-time, though
   It is Spring-like, my throat keeps flooding:
Peep soft at my mate, – she is there below, –
   Where the bramble trails are budding.

VIII

'She sits on the nest and she never stirs;
   She is true to the trust I gave her;
And what were my love if I cheered not hers
   As long as my throat can quaver?'

Alfred Austin (1835–1913)

31ˢᵀ MAY

The Birds and the Flowers

FROM *MILTON*, BOOK 2, PLATE 31, LINES 46–63

Thou perceivest the Flowers put forth their
    precious Odours;
And none can tell how from so small a centre
    comes such sweet,
Forgetting that within that centre Eternity expands
Its ever-during doors, that Og and Anak fiercely
    guard.
First, ere the morning breaks, joy opens in the
    flowery bosoms,
Joy even to tears, which the Sun rising dries: first
    the Wild Thyme
And Meadow-sweet, downy and soft, waving
    among the reeds,
Light springing on the air, lead the sweet dance;
    they wake
The Honeysuckle sleeping on the oak; the flaunting
    beauty
Revels along upon the wind; the White-thorn,
    lovely May,

Opens her many lovely eyes; listening the Rose
    still sleeps –
None dare to wake her; soon she bursts her crimson –
    curtain'd bed
And comes forth in the majesty of beauty. Every
    Flower,
The Pink, the Jessamine, the Wallflower, the
    Carnation,
The Jonquil, the mild Lily opes her heavens; every
    Tree
And Flower and Herb soon fill the air with an
    innumerable dance,
Yet all in order sweet and lovely. Men are sick with
    love!
Such is the Vision of the lamentation of Beulah
    over Ololon.

William Blake (1757–1827)

Index of first lines

Index of poets

Acknowledgements

As always, a huge thanks to everyone at Hatchards for looking after my books so well.

Thanks to all my friends who made recommendations and especially Joel Knight who wrote a poem for this anthology. At Batsford Nicola Newman, Tina Persaud and Lilly Phelan are wonderful editors and make compiling these anthologies a joy.

For curious readers, Matilda is a small grey tabby cat who went missing for three months during the winter whilst I was compiling the original anthology from which this collection is taken. Without Mat and Sarah, it would have been a much harder time. Happily, by spring she had been rescued and resumed her duties as my paperweight.

Permissions

W H Auden, 'Ten Songs:V', from *Collected Shorter Poems 1927-1957*. Reprinted by permission of Curtis Brown, Ltd.

David Austin, 'A Flower of the Himalayas' and 'Soil', from *The Breathing Earth*, Enitharmon Press, 2014. Reprinted with permission of David Austin Roses.

Edmund Blunden, 'Spring Night', from Edmund Blunden: Selected Poems, Carcanet Press, 1982. Reprinted by permission of Carcanet Press Limited.

Patrick Dickinson, 'Bluebells', from *Poets of Our Time*, J. Murray, 1965. Reprinted with permission of Penguin Random House.

T S Eliot, 'Little Gidding', from *Four Quartets*, Faber & Faber, 2001. Reprinted with permission of Faber & Faber.

Eleanor Farjeon, 'March, You Old Blusterer' and 'Nightpiece', from *The Children's Bells*, Oxford University Press, 1973. Reprinted by kind permission of David Higham Associates Ltd.

Joel Knight, 'Night'. With kind permission of Joel Knight.

Philip Larkin, 'The Trees', from High Windows, Faber & Faber, 2003. Reprinted with permission of Faber & Faber.